The Field Place
Mystery

"The Field Place Mystery" is an original idea by the author Graham Lelliott. It looks into the rumours, research and personal memories regarding the top secret wartime tunnels and underground command centre believed to be below Field Place in Worthing, West Sussex, which is allegedly still protected by a 73 year government secrecy rule.

Graham Lelliott

The Field Place Mystery

10 Digit ISBN 0-9553893-1-3
13 Digit ISBN 978-0-9553893-1-3

Published by;
Graham Lelliott, 3 Busticle Lane, Sompting,
Lancing, West Sussex, BN15 0DH, England
Website: www.grahamlelliott.co.uk

Printed and bound in 2007 by;
CPI Antony Rowe, 48-50 Birch Close,
Eastbourne, East Sussex, BN23 6PE, England
Tel: + 44 (0)1323 434700
Website: www.antonyrowe.co.uk

This book is dedicated to my grandfather, Eric (Jack) Kennard, who passed away in August 2007. He was a kind, humorous and inspiring man, who will always be remembered.

Contents

Introduction

Field Place is an area of land located in Durrington to the west of Worthing in West Sussex. My interest in Field Place first grew when my grandmother found an article on the front page of the Worthing Herald on Friday 5th January 1996.

The article, written by news editor John Hammond, explained that two men, Ken Harris and John Hammersley, had been researching a top secret, wartime underground command centre and vast labyrinth of tunnels around Field Place in Worthing. During this time my fascination with the Second World War was growing and so my grandmother cut out the article for me. I read it with great concentration and interest.

Over the years a handful of articles continued to be published and these were added to my library. I had become increasingly interested in the mystery of Field Place and so I tried my utmost to get in contact with the two researchers, Ken Harris and John Hammersley. Sadly this was not possible. It was now evident that if I wanted to find out more, I would have to research the subject myself.

Over ten years later, research on this underground complex has been difficult. Letters, emails and copies of the newspaper articles, have been sent to many organisations, including the Ministry of Defence, which incidentally have denied its existence. Visits to the National Archives at Kew, West Sussex Records Office at Chichester and Field Place itself have also resulted in disappointment. Many phone calls have been made and much time and money wasted.

Many claim to have been down these tunnels although to this day no official documents have been seen. As a result of this it is hoped that by compiling this publication, it may spark new interest, uncover many unsolved mysteries and raise more support in the future.

Graham Lelliott

The Field Place Estate

The Field Place estate was once a much larger area of land than it is today. It was first mentioned in the 11th century and was originally owned by the Cooke family, who lived on the site for over 300 years.

After the Cooke family the Westbrooke – Richardson's owned the site, before passing it on to the Henty family during the mid to late 1700's. The present house was built in the 18th century and as the Henty's were very successful farming and business people, they used some of their wealth to upgrade the house into a fine Georgian residence. The Henty's are responsible for the present house frontage.

The 18th century house. (Authors Collection)

During the agricultural depression the Henty's revenue declined and the family emigrated to Australia. E. W. Margerson became the new owner until 1909 when Alfred Bates purchased the site, who paid £250,000 on house renovations. When Alfred died the house became the Manor Country Club.

During the Second World War, Field Place was requisitioned by the Air Ministry under the War Emergencies Act 1939. Current records state that Field Place was used between 1942 and 1945 as the domestic site for the nearby GCI (Ground Control Interception) radar station at RAF Durrington.

After the war, the site then became the Flamingo Country Club and in 1956 Worthing Borough Council purchased the site for £17,500 where many improvements were made. The original flint barn, dating back to 1773 was refurbished and reopened in 1988 as the ideal venue for wedding receptions, seminars, plays, dances, etc.

The flint barn, dating back to 1773. (Authors Collection)

The main house was refurbished in 1989, which revealed much of the original oak panelling and stonework. The site today offers, 6 floodlit tennis courts, 4 bowling greens, 4 netball courts, 2 petanque pistes, table tennis, a putting green, conference rooms and the art centre barn theatre.

Field Place is also the home of the Worthing and District Society of Model Engineers who have a 440 yard elevated triple gauge (5, 3½ and 2½ inch) railway line, complete with a short tunnel, footbridge and station/clubhouse.

In July 2000, and to mark the 60th anniversary of GCI Durrington, a plaque was unveiled in the 18th century house to acknowledge the buildings use during the war. The Royal Air Force Air Defence Radar Museum were present and noted that; "Sixty years ago the first of the original six "hand made" Ground Control Interception (GCI) stations was installed in the countryside on the outskirts of Worthing, Sussex. Before the war that part of the countryside had been earmarked for development and an infrastructure of roads had been laid down.

However, the onset of war in 1939 brought a halt to the development, and the new radar station was well endowed with roads criss-crossing the site. The mobile GCI at Durrington was later replaced with an intermediate, and then a 'Final' GCI in 1942, complete with its "Happidrome" operations block. The domestic site for the unit was centred on the nearby Field Place, a two-storey 18th century country house, which became the messes and airman's accommodation, the Officers and WAAFs being billeted in nearby houses.

Since the war, considerable building has been carried out in the area, now absorbed by Worthing and it is hard to believe that RAF Durrington was surrounded by green fields in 1941. In 1953 the "Happidrome" was converted into a school as the main building of Palatine School.

To commemorate the founding of the first GCI at Durrington, two plaques, the vision of a former Durrington radar mechanic Mr Gordon Smith, and produced by Sqn Ldr Mike Dean RAF (Rtd) of the Historical Radar Archive, were unveiled on the Operations Site and the Domestic Site on Friday 21st July 2000. Gordon Smith sincerely felt that the role of RAF Durrington and the personnel who served there during the Second World War should be remembered in this Millennium Year.

Twelve ex-Durrington personnel, RAF and WAAF, were welcomed to the site in bright sunshine by the Deputy Headmaster, Mick Baldwin, before handing over to Gordon Smith for a resume of the history of RAF Durrington. The Mayor of Worthing and Councillor Ann Lynn then unveiled the first plaque.

The company were then invited to tour the "Happidrome", converted to a school building by the expediency of painting over the raw 1942 brickwork of the internal walls with bright colours and installing some windows and extra internal walls. The Dorman Long steel joists in the roof were clearly visible. The result was a light and airy building, a vast improvement on other "Happidromes" in other places, which are used as farmer's hay stores.

The company then moved onto the former domestic site where the Lady Mayor unveiled the second plaque in Field Place, now owned by Worthing Borough Council as part of their Community Services. After the ceremony a buffet luncheon was served in the dinning room, and on display were many personal photographs of the old days, of green fields, and young men and women whom 60 years had not yet touched. Many stories were told, of stirring events, unhappily of people who are long since gone, but of others of whom the memory is bright."

The plaque, unveiled at Field Place is seen here. As one can see it is well looked after and polished regularly, so much so that the reflection on the plaque shown in the photograph makes it difficult to read. The plaque reads; Royal Air Force Durrington 1940 – 1945. 1942 – Field Place – 1945. To the memory of all personnel of the Royal Air Force, Women's Auxiliary Air Force and commonwealth Forces who served on the Ground Control of Interception Radar and used this historic building as their living quarters during World War 2. (Authors Collection)

In the Public Eye

As explained in the introduction, there has over the years, been a handful of newspaper articles on the alleged wartime complex. The subject has therefore not been forgotten but has remained very much in the public eye. Due to the lack of evidence, and having had full support from the Worthing Herald, the West Sussex Gazette and the Worthing Argus and Sentinel, it has been agreed to republish all articles on this subject as they originally appeared in the paper.

On Friday 5th January, the Worthing Herald published the first article on the subject. Titled "Secret Under Your Feet" it sparked much interest and explained the following; "Worthing may be sitting on top of a major tourist attraction – a top secret, wartime underground command centre and vast labyrinth of tunnels around Field Place. Even now, the whereabouts of the main entrances are covered by a 73-year secrecy rule but the tunnel network has been charted by enthusiasts.

Mr Ken Harris says buried beneath the ground in bombproof concrete was a radar headquarters, plus the local base for government in the event of invasion or other disaster. Mr Harris, brother of Field Place amenity complex manager, Tony, said, 'It was top secret – when the soldiers and sentries went down from the main entrance, which was within the Field Place manor house, they were not allowed in any of the other passageways, only where their duties allowed them to go. Nobody knew what everyone else was doing apart from the base's operators.'

The tunnels were far more complex than Mr Harris initially thought, with several levels and one stretching from the eastern side of West Park, where the children's play area is, to Field Place. From there they went to the Durrington railway station area, the Strand, a military hospital set up at what is now the Inland Revenue's Barrington Road site, and to what used to be an above ground radar base, where Palatine School is today.

Field Place green keeper John Hammersley said he explored the tunnels as a child in the 1950's – before they were sealed off. 'They were that big you could ride a bike through them.' Mr Hammersley added, 'The main command centre was under the putting area at Field Place and that's still there.' The RAF's concrete tunnels also linked with old, brick built ones, believed to have been used in the days of smuggling.

Mr Harris said research at the government's war records office revealed there were a number of rooms under Field Place's putting ground, bowling greens and tennis courts – all about 19ft below the surface. The main command centre was about 23ft wide by 40ft long.

Digs had exposed a wartime well, an emergency water storage tank, the main transport entrance and pillars, believed to have been part of a covered entranceway. Mr Clive Swonnell, Worthing branch chairman of the Federation of Small Businesses, said, 'I would love to see the place opened up as a tourist attraction.'

Two weeks later on Friday 19th January 1996, another article about the subject appeared on page 8. Although similar to the first article, this went into greater detail. Titled "Hidden But Not Forgotten: Towns Underground Secrets", news editor John Hammond wrote; "History enthusiasts have been tracing the network of tunnels under Field Place, Worthing – a labyrinth that led to a secret wartime base. Ken Harris, brother of Field Place amenity complex manager, Tony, said, 'When we first came here about 30 years ago, we used to have the radar reunion people here for their annual meetings.

'They always used to talk about the radar headquarters and the "local seat of government" being here. Then our ears pricked up when they talked of underground tunnels. 'Other people talked about how big the tunnels were – "six miles of tunnels" – and that just before D-Day they stored 500 Harley-Davidsons down there before going over to occupied France.'

Mr Harris said it turned out a green keeper at Field Place, Mr John Hammersley, had played in the tunnels as a boy in the 1950's. 'They were vastly more complicated than we first thought,' said Mr Harris. They stretched from the eastern side of West Park, where the children's play area is, to Field Place. From there, they went to the Durrington railway station area, The Strand, a military hospital set up at what is now the Inland Revenue's Barrington Road site, and what used to be an above ground radar base, where Palatine School is today.

The council blocked off the concrete tunnels to prevent vandalism. 'The man who did it has now retired and gone to that council in the sky.' Efforts to try and trace the labyrinth have included consulting a well-known dowser from London, who said there was so much under the putting green and bowling areas he could not get a clear reading.

Further research at the Governments war records office was also useful. A sketch of the radar room is shown here. However, even now the whereabouts of the main entrances is covered by a 73-year secrecy rule.

The radar room – a sketch showing the equipment used.

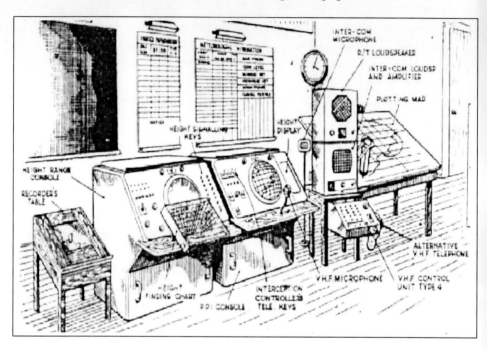

Mr Harris said Worthing Borough Council had been very good and allowed exploratory digs to take place, but some rooms were about 19ft under the surface. 'We know where everything is – really it's now just trying to find someone who could tell us where there might have been inspection shafts, which would be only two or three feet under the surface, or air vents.'

The main command centre, under the putting area at Field Place, was about 23ft wide by 40ft long. Digs had exposed a wartime well, an emergency water storage tank, the main transport entrance and pillars, believed to have been part of a covered entranceway. 'I think the people of Worthing really don't realise how big a part the town played in the war – when you think we were the first radar station of this sort in the country and everything was copied from this. 'I think Worthing people should be proud the town played such a part in the war. Unfortunately, it was so secret that not many people know about it.'

Soldiers and sentries at the base were allowed only where their duties allowed them and the only people who knew what everyone else was doing were the base's operators.

Mr Hammersley, who played in the tunnels when he was about 12, said there was a route into the tunnels through rooms in Field Place's manor house. He had also seen evidence of the RAF's concrete tunnels linking with old brick built ones, believed to have been used in the days of smuggling."

Digging into history – John Hammersley and Ken Harris.
(Worthing Herald and Gazette)

It is worth noting that "the radar room" sketch shown in the previous article is in fact a sketch of the Interception Controllers Room to be found in a Happidrome and is not related to the alleged underground complex at Field Place.

The same page contained a second article, titled "We Decided to Explore", which explained; "The Herald's recent front-page story revealing there was a labyrinth of secret, underground tunnels under Field Place, Worthing, brought back childhood memories for Hugh Bartlett. History enthusiasts told how tunnels led to a wartime radar headquarters, plus the local base for government in the event of an invasion or other disaster.

But after the war and when Mr Bartlett was about six years old, he knew the tunnels as a 'secret' play area. 'I know there's a huge network underneath there.' Mr Bartlett, now 51 and living in Littlehampton, added, 'We hadn't been told there were tunnels underneath there, but, kids being what they are, we decided to explore.'

Mr Bartlett used to live in one of the four houses, which stood in Bolsover Road after the war – the rest of the area was surrounded by fields. 'Before it was Field Place, it was a country club called the Flamingo and there was a family called the Posfords who owned it. They had two boys and my brother and I were friendly with them.'

The lads use to get into the labyrinth through what may have been a ventilation shaft in front of Field Place. He said this was like a little coalbunker raised above the ground with a small, steel door on it. 'We went down onto a staircase and into the tunnel. There are lots of little annexes down there. It was something like the underground hospital in Jersey – like a honeycomb, with lots of bits and pieces.'

Mr Bartlett said as a child some of the areas seemed 'really spooky,' so they never went in them, but he did recall a large room. 'The thing I remember distinctly was the great big, thick steel tables.' Also in the network were old-fashioned fire extinguishers hanging on walls, old bicycles in one of the annexe rooms and large light fittings in the tunnels.

Mr Bartlett's mother, Jean, who still lives in Bolsover Road, said she had no idea her son was exploring the tunnels. Four generations of Mrs Bartlett's family have lived in Worthing, but she recalled the public were not allowed into the area around Field Place during the war."

The Argus published a letter on 20th February 2001 from Worthing resident Mrs B. M. Bashford who gave her own views on the subject. Titled "Dropping In", She explained, "I recalled something my son told me several years ago, when he and some school pals used to enter what he called an air raid shelter and play. They got into the bunker through a hole and dropped into what he described as a large room. There were apparently other exits from this room, which had been bricked up, so I think there is a secret maze.

The area with the entrance is behind the running track at Worthing Sports Centre, near the children's play area. I hope this is of interest to you, and I would be interested to hear of any other stories of the underground maze. My son is now in his early thirties and I called him to verify his story."

After many years of silence, excitement struck on Wednesday 14th February 2007, whilst reading the West Sussex Gazette, when I discovered an article about a concrete structure, which was found in a back garden near Field Place and was believed to be linked with the underground complex.

Titled "Hidden But Not Forgotten: Town's Underground Secrets" Jeannie Knight wrote; "There may be a new lead on a network of secret tunnels, which lie beneath Worthing. A West Sussex Gazette reader has alerted the newspaper to the existence of a concrete structure in a back garden at a significant site near Field Place in the town, which she believes may well be linked to the secret tunnel complex.

It is close to the Inland Revenue's Barrington Road site, which was formally 'The Strand', a military hospital from which the tunnels are believed to have stretched to the eastern side of West Park, to Durrington railway station and to an above ground radar station where Palatine School is today. The council blocked off the concrete tunnels some years ago, to prevent vandalism.

The nature of the tunnels was last investigated 10 years ago, when two history enthusiasts, John Hammersley and Ken Harris were given permission by Worthing Borough Council to undertake some exploratory digs around Field Place. Although they plotted out the course of much of the labyrinth of tunnels, details, such as the whereabouts of the main entrance are still protected by a 73-year government secrecy rule.

The main command centre is believed to be under the putting green at Field Place, some 20 feet below the surface, and measuring 23ft wide by 40ft long. The digs also exposed a wartime well, an emergency water storage tank, the main transport entrance and pillars, believed to have been part of a covered entranceway.

But much is still not known about the subterranean complex, which is reputed, to extend up to six miles. Children are known to have played in some of the structures after the war, and some of them have contacted the press describing the tunnels as "a honeycomb with lots of bits and pieces" and "like the underground hospital in Jersey."

The tunnels appear to have been accessed by the children through ventilation shafts with steel doors, and then via staircases. Mr Harris, one of the amateur historians who researched the tunnels, said: "I think the people of Worthing really don't realise how big a part the town played in the war – when you think we were the first radar station of this sort in the country and everything was copied from this. People should be proud of the part the town played, but unfortunately, it was so secret that not many people know about it.

"Soldiers and sentries at the base were allowed only where there duties allowed them and the only people who knew what everyone else was doing were the base operators." Fellow researcher, Mr Hammersley, played in the tunnels when he was 12 and said, there was a route into the tunnels through rooms in Field Place's manor house. He had also seen evidence of the RAF's concrete tunnels linking with old brick built ones, believed to have been used in the days of smuggling."

The concrete structure. (The West Sussex Gazette)

Having found the location of this "concrete structure", it was my intention to investigate to establish whether this was an entrance to the underground complex or perhaps, quite simply a Second World War air raid shelter, which are still very common in back gardens across southern England. Due to the landowner's wishes, this was not possible.

On Thursday 15th February 2007, Paul Holden at the Worthing Argus wrote an article in the Sentinel about the rumours circulating in the town regarding smugglers tunnels. Field Place was also mentioned but still there was no new evidence. Titled "Rumours Abound In Worthing", he wrote; "Rumours abound in Worthing, especially about historic tunnels under the town, but the Sentinel takes them with a liberal pinch of salt.

For years, we were led to believe that smugglers used tunnels leading from the seafront to the cellar of the Thieves Kitchen (formerly the Vintners Arms and latterly the Vintners Parrott), and also from this hostelry, under Warwick Street, to the Warwick pub.

The Sentinel was, some years ago, given a tour of the cellars, which are admittedly very old and atmospheric, but found no convincing evidence for tunnels. It is also claimed that a tunnel formerly linked Broadwater Manor with St Mary's Church before continuing on to Charmandean. Again unproven.

Some say the area around Field Place is a rabbit warren of subterranean passages dating back to the Second World War, when the area was taken over by the military. But nobody has yet found them, or the Army equipment, including many a Harley Davidson motorcycle, said to have been hidden inside. There is, however, a tunnel under Broadwater Green – a former air raid shelter now used by fire fighters for training."

Research, Rumours and Personal Memories

Over the years the managers at Field Place have also tried to look into what may be below their feet and it seems as though they have been given the same headache as me. They have sent many letters to various organisations, including the Ministry of Defence, all of which have also resulted in disappointment.

The letter of response from the Ministry of Defence is probably the most interesting, which stated that Field Place has no wartime tunnels and an underground command centre. Curiously the organisation then contradicted itself by saying that if blocked off entrances are uncovered, under no circumstances should they be tampered with as it would certainly lead to serious implications.

The entire site has been gone over with a fine toothcomb and no concealed entranceways have been found, not even in the cellar below the house. It has been said on numerous occasions that the main entrance to the underground complex was located at the west end of the putting green. I am told that this entranceway was filled in shortly after the war and a tree planted in its position.

X marks the spot. The site of the alleged main entrance. (Authors Collection)

A diagram drawn by an Elizabeth Sullivan also supports this entrance location and stated that this entrance was the only way in and out of the underground complex. This diagram, to be found in the history file at Field Place, shows an outline of a rather large room below a majority of the site.

To confuse matters there is absolutely no mention of any tunnels, making me wonder whether all these rumours may just lead to what is simply a very large air raid shelter for the service men who stayed in the 18th century house during the war. If not a shelter, perhaps an underground store room?

The diagram was drawn in 1995 and it is unclear what connection Elizabeth Sullivan has with Field Place. Suffice to say, no contact details had been left, leaving her completely untraceable.

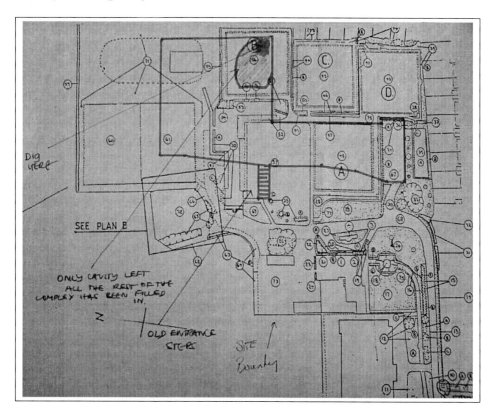

The diagram is seen here and clearly shows the main entrance with steps.
(Elizabeth Sullivan / Worthing Borough Council)

An aerial photograph of the site, also kept in the history file at Field Place, certainly shows distinct lines and right-angled markings below the surface of the putting green. This photograph is seen below and shows the putting green in the centre. Due to the quality of the reproduction, these "distinct lines and right-angled markings" are sadly not very clear. (Bill Newman)

Many ex servicemen who were based at RAF Durrington and who stayed at Field Place (the domestic site for the radar station) have been contacted and questioned about the alleged tunnels and underground command centre. This subject has been dismissed as rubbish.

With this in mind it could be that they are right. It could also mean that they were unaware of what was going on below their feet and even if they were aware of this underground complex, they most certainly would have been told not to disclose this information.

Field Place management and staff have been told that the underground complex was constructed by the 172 Tunnelling Company Royal Engineers, who incidentally were also involved with constructing, among others, the once top secret navel tunnels (HMS Forward) at South Heighton, East Sussex in 1941.

Tunnels of this type were also constructed at Newhaven Fort, East Sussex at around the same time. At this entrance the visitor information plaque states that similar tunnels were also constructed by the 172 Tunnelling Company Royal Engineers at Shaftsbury Avenue in Worthing.

Interestingly, Shaftsbury Avenue is a stone's throw away from Field Place and so this rumour may well not be too far from the truth. Sadly, there is no record of any tunnels in Shaftsbury Avenue, not even with the Royal Engineers Museum in Gillingham, Kent.

Other research has found evidence of over 200 phone lines entering the Field Place manor house, which makes one highly curious.

It had also been noted that Sky Television had approached Worthing Borough Council to film a documentary about the mysteries surrounding Field Place but strangely enough were turned away. The power of television and even the power of the television company itself may have uncovered many mysteries and may have answered many questions if they had been given permission.

Council Management carried on with the research until, in a letter sent to Field Place, dated 23rd March 2001, John Thorpe, the Assistant Director of Community Services for Worthing Borough Council, stated; "Unfortunately, it is apparent that we are not going to get very far with our inquiries, and I would propose, at this stage not to pursue the matter any further."

During my research I had the opportunity to speak to a handful of local people who had either been in these tunnels, or were aware of other tunnels in the area, which may have been related to the alleged Field Place underground complex.

Peter Reeves explained; "I was employed as an engineer at Worthing Borough Council from 1974 to 1996 and worked on many engineer contracts in the town. While undertaking research on underground plant and drainage for the new bowling green in the 1980's, plans held in the old drawing filling room at the Town Hall contained plans from the 1920's (?) which indicated an underground passage from Field Place complex to the old barn. I do not know if these plans were retained when the engineering group was transferred to Portland House in the 1990's."

Gerald Tiller also has knowledge of the tunnels and said; "I worked for the corporation as a joiner and carpenter for 33 years. When the council bought Field Place, the house was renovated. Builders and plumbers were below in the cellar when a wall collapsed, revealing the tunnel entrance. I was desperate to go in so I got a torch and climbed into the tunnel. It was completely dry in there and measured roughly 5ft x 6ft. There was no oxygen in there and I was becoming short of breath so I decided to retreat. The site foreman demanded it be bricked back up again and from that nothing else was said."

David Bowdrey stated; "The entrance was in the south east corner of the Field Place complex. It had been boarded up but my friend and I, Geoff Sanderson, managed to get in. The tunnel led towards the Bolsover Road direction and I recall there being another tunnel on the left about 15 metres in. It was obviously very dark in there and being kids we were too frightened to go any further, so we came out."

Pearl O'Connor said she played under Field Place as a child in the late 1940's. She said; "Us girls didn't go in that far, as we were scared and knew it was out of bounds, but there was definitely something there."

Peter Bailey said a late work colleague of his once told of how she found a mysterious underground passageway. He said; "She worked at Field Place and was often sent up to Littlehampton Road to deliver parcels to a guard station, but on one occasion it was unmanned. She went inside but to her surprise there was not an office, but a steep staircase. She started to go down but was stopped and severely reprimanded."

An Alternative View

Whilst gathering information, I was fortunate to be put in contact with military researcher Bob Jenner of Horsham, West Sussex. He had an incredible knowledge of Second World War and Cold War manmade underground structures, but also radar installations. Mr Jenner was kind enough to look into my research and spent much of his valuable time compiling the following;

"Following Germany's change of tactics from daylight to night bombing subsequent to the Battle of Britain, the 'Night Interception Committee's' meeting of 19th August 1940 proposed that a radar receiver in a mobile, miniature operations room would provide efficient ground control to enable fighters equipped with Air Intercept (AI) radar, already in existence, and capable of cover over both sea and land. The Royal Aircraft Establishment (RAE) was instructed to design and to provide an example within one month with the title of ground Control Interception (GCI).

In urgent response, the scientific services threw everything they had at the problem resulting in a hurriedly cobbled together, mobile intercept unit based upon a War Office 'gunlaying' equipment designed at the Air Defence Research and Development Establishment (ADRDE) at Christchurch near Bournemouth, incorporating modifications by the Air Ministry's Telecommunications Research Establishment (TRE) at Worth Matravers, near Swanage.

The experimental model of this, the first GCI was ready by 10th October 1940 and was sited in the open fields of Field Place Estate at Durrington, on the northwest outskirts of Worthing, which had previously been requisitioned by the War Office. The estate had been prepared for redevelopment before the war and had roads and services, gas, water, electricity and sewage laid on.

The GCI unit consisted of two aerial trailers, one each for Transmitting (Tx) and one for Receiving (Rx), A truck held the actual transmitter whilst a second truck held the receiver and the operations room. Two trailer generators and two mobile vhf communications vehicles completed the technical equipment; all laid out in a long line on what is now Palatine Road.

The success of this installation: RAF Durrington GCI Station No 01G was swiftly followed by a prototype station at RAF Sopley (02G) and then four more production models. The title of these stations was Air Ministry

Experimental Station Type 8 (AMES Type 8). Plans were drawn up for a permanent fixed installation capable of multi-interceptions called AMES Type 7 housed in a brick built operations room entitled a 'Happidrome'. A delay in the design and equipping of these resulted in a series of intermediate mobile and transportable stations being utilised. Durrington continued to be used as an experimental as well as an operational station with Sopley as the prototype site.

Having established the station the first requirement was for accommodation for personnel, The Air Ministry acquired from the War Office the use of Manor House Country Club (Field Place House) and its grounds laid out for sport, tennis courts and bowling greens etc, which was vacant and this became the HQ of the Domestic Site with offices and mess within the house, whilst huts were provided near the garages to the north of the house for other ranks.

Four large detached houses in Bolsover Road (the only properties in the road) were included and were used as Officers Mess and WAAF's quarters. Two cottages and other outbuildings were utilised for stores and M/T. Extensive private wire telephone lines from the Private Branch Exchange (PBX) in the Happidrome were routed through Field Place House to the railway bridge at Durrington Station and thence to Worthing Trunk Telephone Exchange in Mulberry Lane three-quarters of a mile away.

RAF Durrington continued as a successful GCI radar station until the end of the war when it was closed and the equipment removed. The Happidrome building at the technical site remained and later became a school, now greatly enlarged but still based upon the original structure.

By 1945 the owners of Field Place Estate including Field Place House and sports facilities, and the four houses in Bolsover Road, put it up for auction in 35 lots, pending derequisition by the War Office, although still occupied by the Air Ministry. The auction took place on 25th September 1945. The house and sporting facilities were purchased by what became the 'Flamingo Country Club. A detailed description of the lots, the buildings and facilities exist today. No mention of any underground features is included in this accurate description of the lot.

In 1956 Field Place, the pre-war Manor House Country Club and post-war Flamingo Country Club, auctioned as one lot, was purchased by Worthing Council for a Sports and Leisure Centre, a situation that remains to this day. Improvements were made during 1956 and the house was refurbished in 1989.

Move forward twenty years to the mid 1960's and rumours start to appear regarding a secret underground headquarters at Field Place. Then at the beginning of January 1996 an article appears in the Worthing Herald consolidating these rumours with the result that on 19th January 1996 a major feature appeared in the paper.

Where to start? Let's look at the secrecy claim. "Field Place records are closed for 73 years" This is a misread of the Public Records (now National Archives) closure rules, which are in multiples of 25 years, i.e. 25, 50, 75 and 100 years from the date the file closed.

All records held at the National Archives are catalogued, noting the current status of the file, ie, Open, Closed (with the period of closure shown) or retained by Department of Origin. If a record is not listed in the catalogue, it does not exist in the Archive and if it does not exist it cannot be closed for 75 years.

An inspection of the records held by Worthing Council at Field Place was made. Prominent among them are dozens of letters to every possible department of Government, local and national as well as record offices and libraries. However all the letters were the same, only the addressees differed and all the responses were in the same tenor, we have no record, We have no knowledge. This was because the question asked for records of "Field Place" and no such entity existed. As far as the RAF, the wartime occupier of Field Place was concerned, the question should have been " What records exist with regard to RAF Durrington?" as Field Place was only a component of it, namely the domestic site. A search at National Archives for Field Place came back 'No result'.

A further claim is that a reply from the Ministry of Defence stating 'Field Place has no wartime tunnels or an underground command centre' saying that 'if blocked off entrances are uncovered, under no circumstances should they be tampered with as it would certainly lead to serious implications'. This caveat sounds like a sensible caution to add to any enquiry regarding wartime underground structures and would not necessarily be directed at Field Place. Of significance is the fact that this letter is now missing from the file.

A search of the National Archives at Kew came back with 9 files relating to RAF Durrington exclusively and numerous other files where Durrington was mentioned in relation to a technical matter, i.e. radars, experiment, etc.

The station Operations Record Book (ORB), a diary which records daily events operational, technical, personnel, domestic and welfare has not been retained, a normal situation where only the most important percentage of a stations records are kept, in this case the technical records of the first GCI station.

The only underground feature of a Type 7 Final Radar installation is the R7 well, an underground chamber containing the actual transmitter itself, located directly below the aerial, in this case, just to the south of the Happidrome, south of Palatine Road.

Conclusion: There is no secret cover up.

The reference to the sketch of the "Radar Room" (Worthing Herald, Friday 19th January 1996) found in the 'Governments War Records' is in fact an illustration from the Air Force handbook for Final GCI Stations (AP 2901F Final GCI Stations. AMES Type 7) and is of the Blue Intercept Cabin in the Happidrome at what is now Palatine School and not of any underground bunker.

Conclusion: This has no relevance whatsoever.

The main thrust of the story is that of an Underground Radar Headquarters and Local Seat of Government. This, according to a plan in the Field Place records, purports to be over 140 yards long and 40 yards wide. It is supposed to be of three levels with the top some 19 feet below the surface, so we're looking at an underground 3-storey building constructed of concrete in a 5 storey deep excavation. The entrance to this bunker is via the basement of Field Place with up to six miles of tunnels and a 23 feet by 40 feet Command Room. An immense undertaking.

The only two methods of constructing such a building are cut and cover or tunnelling. The former would involve digging an immense pit with sloping sides, constructing a huge 3-storey building and then covering the result with earth, all without any apparent emergency exits, air handling plant or intakes or indeed any noticeable surface features, and all this without anyone noticing. A major problem with this version is that the site was, pre war, laid out as a sports ground with bowling and putting greens and multiple tennis courts, with across the centre of the site a 17th century flint barn (a listed building) and a pavilion. These features were present pre war, during the war, post war and still exist today.

The second method, tunnelling, which would have to have been dug by the Army's Royal Engineers Tunnelling Company and consisted of laying corrugated iron sheets over steel mining hoops, examples of which cover southern England. The tunnelling company responsible for this particular area was 172nd Tunnelling Company, Royal Engineers whose records exist at the National Archives. These show, in detail, a list of all their work, section by section, from the beginning of the war until their redeployment to Gibraltar in 1942. There is no record of any such work at Durrington or Field Place.

A major question at this stage is for whom was this massive bunker built? Not the RAF, who had a strongly built, purpose designed radar station just a couple of hundred yards away, this being the very reason for RAF presence in the first place. The Army wouldn't need it with the RAF in possession of the site nor would the Government, whose graduated dispersal schemes from London are well documented and recorded. An evacuation from London due to an imminent overrun by an enemy would not normally involve a retreat through enemy lines to an area where the invasion had taken place and was occupied by that enemy. The threat of invasion was not fully lifted until the German invasion of Russia in June 1941. The Navy was adequately catered for elsewhere.

Mr Harris, a principal in this story, claimed that the council had given permission for an exploratory dig and that an emergency water tank, a wartime well and the main transport entrance had been uncovered and that they knew where everything was. This is disputed by the council, who state that no permission had ever been applied for, and that even if it had been, the request would have been turned down. Any activity on the site, if indeed any took place at all, would have been un-authorised. Despite this claim, no report, plan, drawing or photograph has been forthcoming and no trace of the alleged artefacts has ever been found.

An examination and a photographic record was made of the basement of Field Place which reveals a double vaulted brick built cellar which had originally contained a wine cellar, a fruit and vegetable store in one vault with a coal cellar in the other. This latter now contains a modern gas-fired central heating boiler. A narrow, now blocked off, staircase led to the then, ground floor kitchen, outside the door of which, an outside stair led back down to the cellar. The 18th century brickwork is intact on all walls with no signs of breaching or blocking up. Some bricks have been removed to facilitate the entry of modern services, such as gas and electricity.

The next claim is of 500 American Harley Davidson motorcycles being stored in the bunker prior to D-Day. These are American machines and were not, under normal circumstances, used by the RAF or British Army. If, in the unlikely event of a US unit not requiring them post D-Day (one questions why they had them at all) then any one of the hundreds of vast US stores and depots across the south and west of the country would have had ample space for these machines and still retained control of them. This part of the story is utterly ludicrous.

The claim that the concrete bunker tunnels link with old brick smuggler tunnels has been investigated and dismissed by others.

Conclusion: There is no primary evidence of any kind to support any of the claims made and which are re-butted above. None of the principal players are either alive or traceable, despite recent press appeals. The remainder is either hearsay or gossip. If any one part of the story falls, so must the rest, which is dependent upon that part.

My contention is that the entire story and its claims are a myth, with the caveat, that only when the site is finally dug up will the truth be fully revealed.

A tentative offer, to the councils Leisure Department, on the behalf of Subterania Britannica (a group within the United Kingdom, who record all underground manmade and man used places), was made; to investigate the alleged bunker by means of excavation was met with the kind, but firm response "Not in a thousand years".

To the reader, Fable or Fact, the choice is yours.

Bob Jenner. July 2007.

Overview

Evidently, much mystery surrounds this subject. My research has, over the years, led to many mixed views. Surprisingly, some of these views have become very heated discussions between individuals who are adamant that Field Place holds a secret and those who believe that the whole subject is a load of rubbish, conceived by imaginative minds.

Many rumours and suggestions have been made. However I hope that the way this publication has been put together, the reader will be interested in the debate.

I would personally like to believe that Field Place played a very large part in supporting the war effort, although until further evidence comes to light, I remain completely open minded about the alleged underground complex.

As a result of this rather large mystery, my research will continue until I am satisfied I have collected all there is to know. Therefore I welcome any comments or additions that may be able to further this subject.

Graham Lelliott

Acknowledgements

My sincere thanks go to the following people, organisations and sources. I would also like to thank those who replied to the Worthing Herald articles on Thursday 20th October 2005, Thursday 31st May 2007 and Thursday 7th June 2007, published to help further this project;

Tim Yates
Mike Franklin
John Hammersley
Ken Harris
Hugh Bartlett
B. M. Bashford
John Hammond
Jeannie Knight
Geoff Ellis
John Buss
Roy Taylor
Bob Jenner
Bill Brooke
Bill Newman
Alan Redman
Phillip Baldock
Martin Mace
Mike Heyworth
Paul Holden
Duncan Robb
John Hellis
Elizabeth Sullivan
Allison Cornell
Norman Langridge
Martin Hayes
Roy Bullers
Bob Chambers
Jane Dore
Peter Bailey
Derek Walker
John Smithbone
Lance Dale
Peter Reeves

Valerie Kay
Mary Lambourne
Gerald Tiller
Steve Buckingham
David Bowdrey
Pearl O'Connor
Edith Heather
Katherine McGlinchey
Worthing Library
Subterranea Britannica
The Argus and Sentinel
Newsquest (Sussex) Ltd
Defence Estates, London
The Pillbox Study Group
The West Sussex Gazette
Worthing Borough Council
Field Place Sports Complex
Ministry of Defence, London
Worthing Herald and Gazette
Imperial War Museum, London
Worthing Museum and Art Gallery
The National Archives, Kew, Surrey
English Heritage, Swindon, Wiltshire
Newhaven Fort, Newhaven, East Sussex
Cabinet Office Openness Team, London
Palatine School, Durrington, West Sussex
Home Office Record Review Team, London
HMS Forward, South Heighton, East Sussex
Royal Engineers Museum, Gillingham, Kent
Council for British Archaeology, Bootham, York
Historic Military Press, Pulborough, West Sussex
Field Place Area Residents Association, Worthing
The West Sussex Records Office, Chichester, West Sussex
County Archaeology, County Hall, Chichester, West Sussex
Worthing and District Society of Model Engineers, Worthing
The Royal Air Force Air Defence Museum, Norwich, Norfolk
Portsmouth Publishing and Printing Ltd, West Sussex Division
MOD Air Historical Branch, RAF Bentley Priory, Stanmore, Middlesex
West Sussex Sites and Monuments Records Team, Chichester, West Sussex